Who Has a Hump?

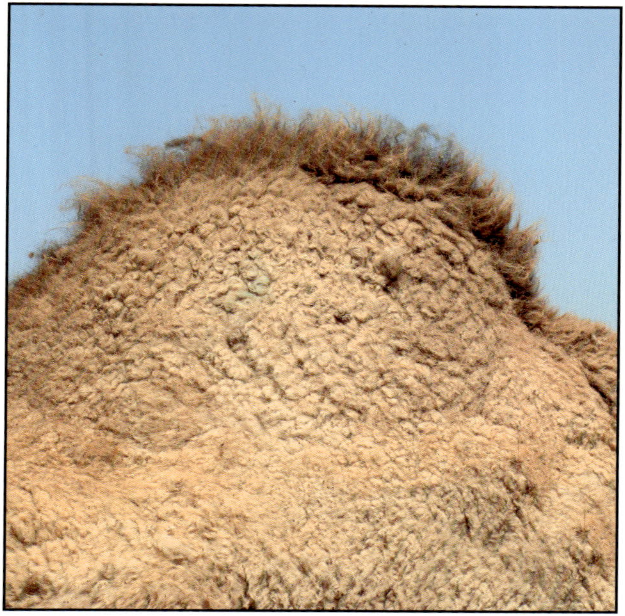

by Kris Bonnell

Look at my feet.

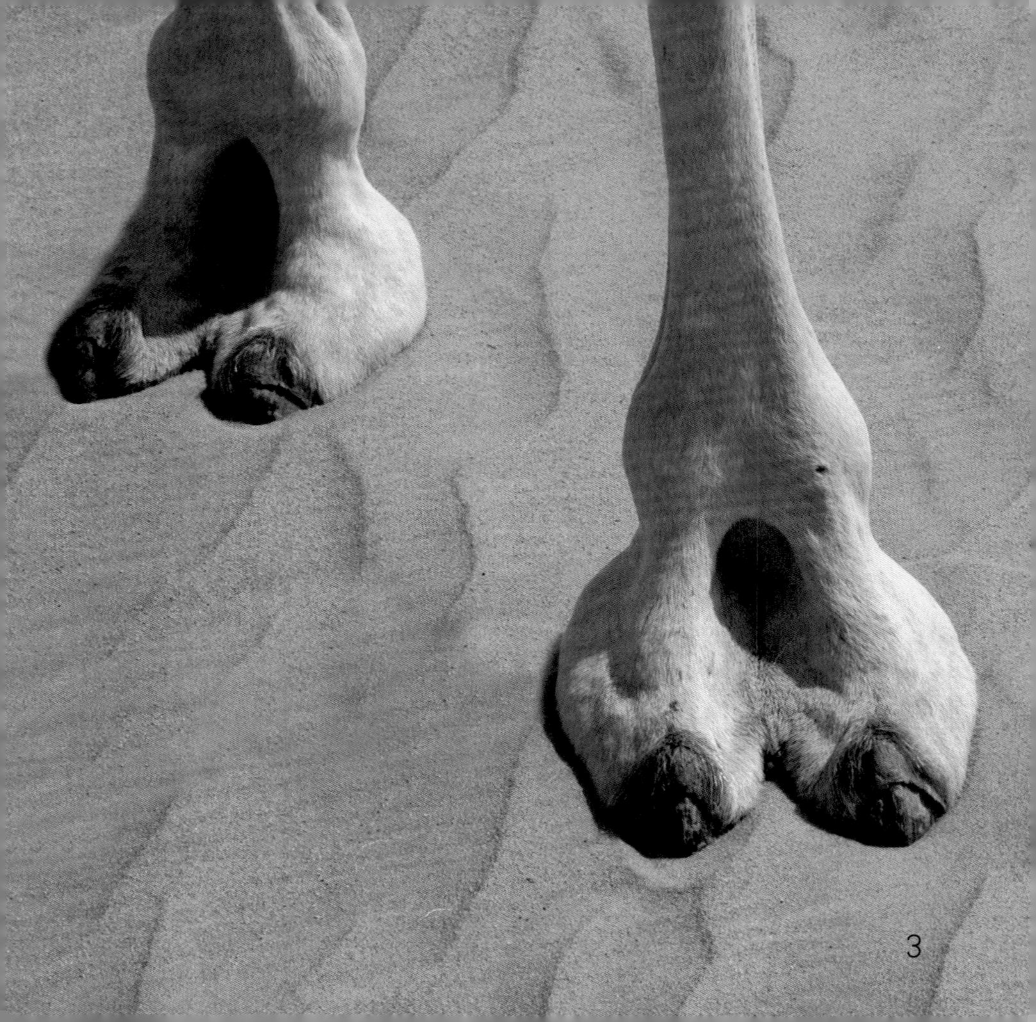

Look at my legs.

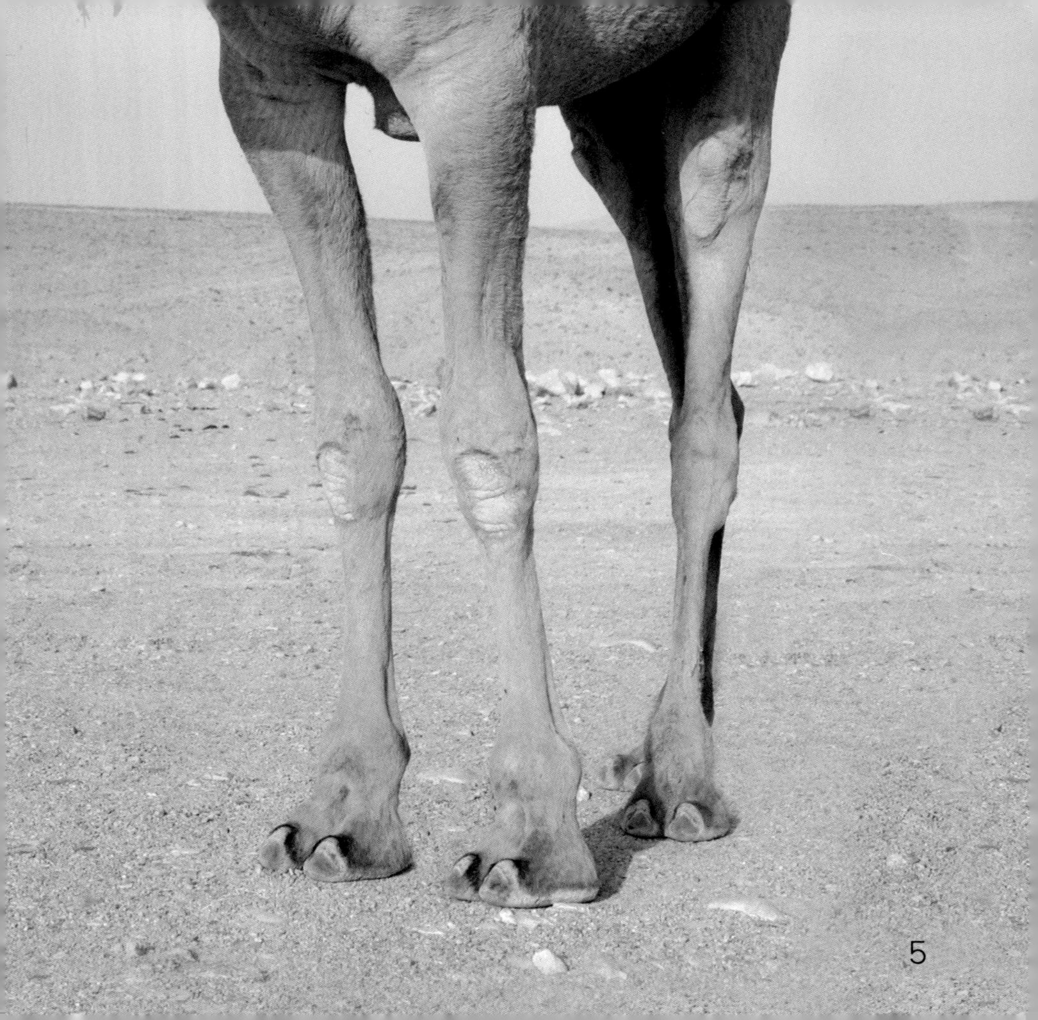

Look at my tail.

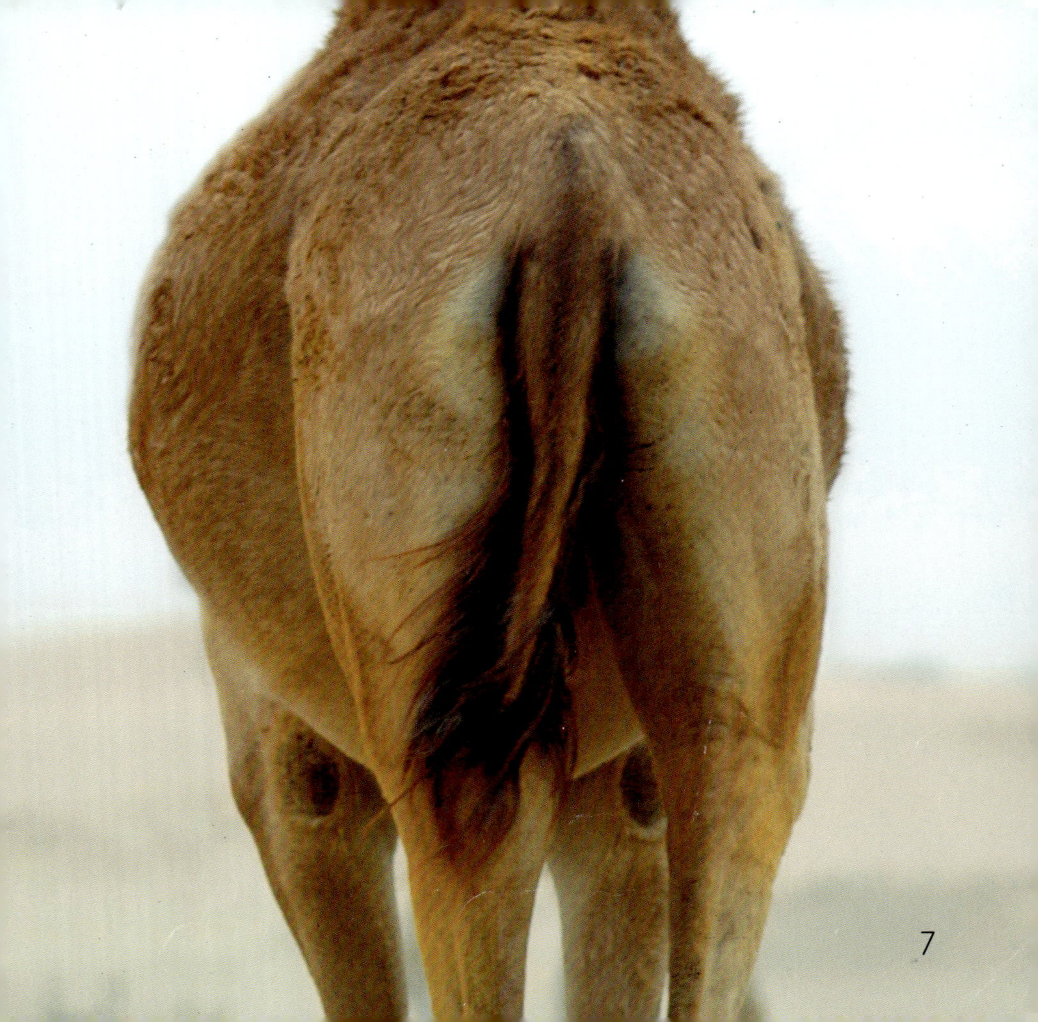

Look at my mouth.

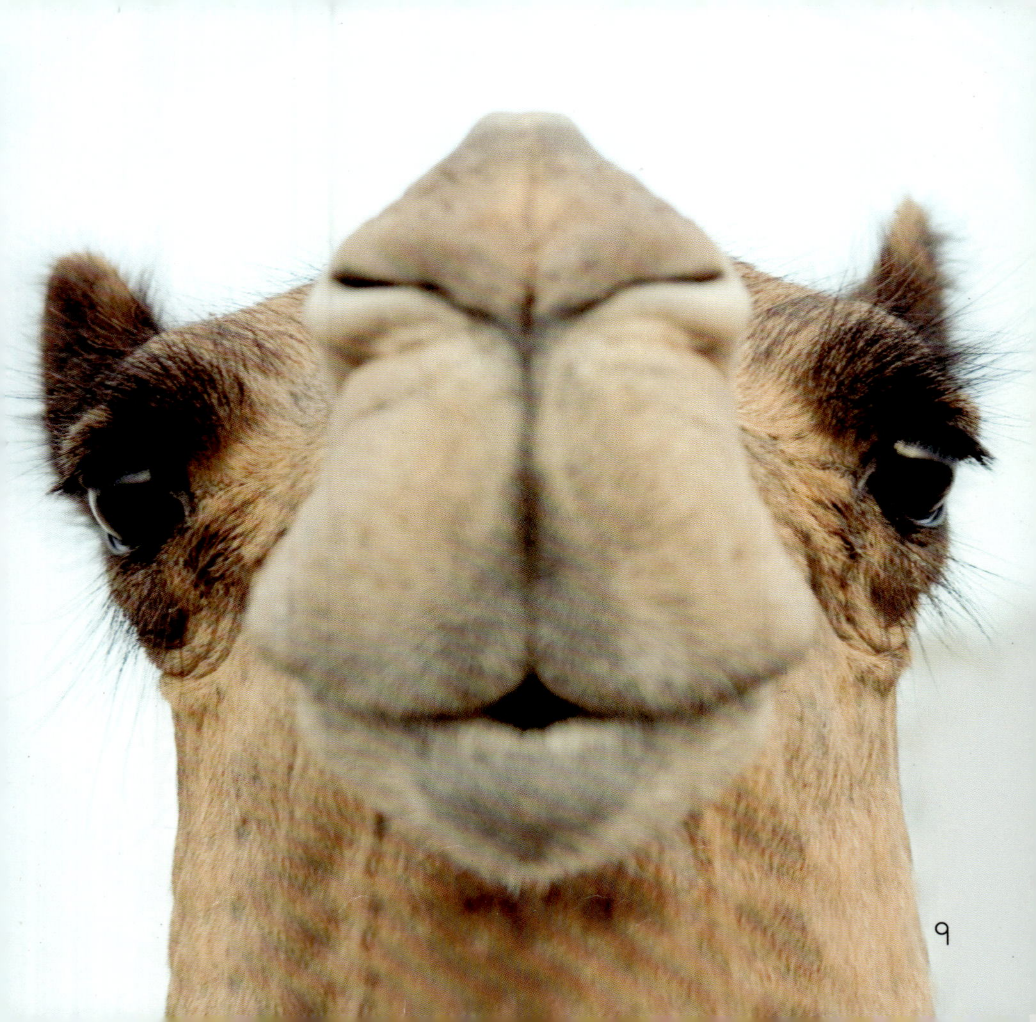

Look at my hump.

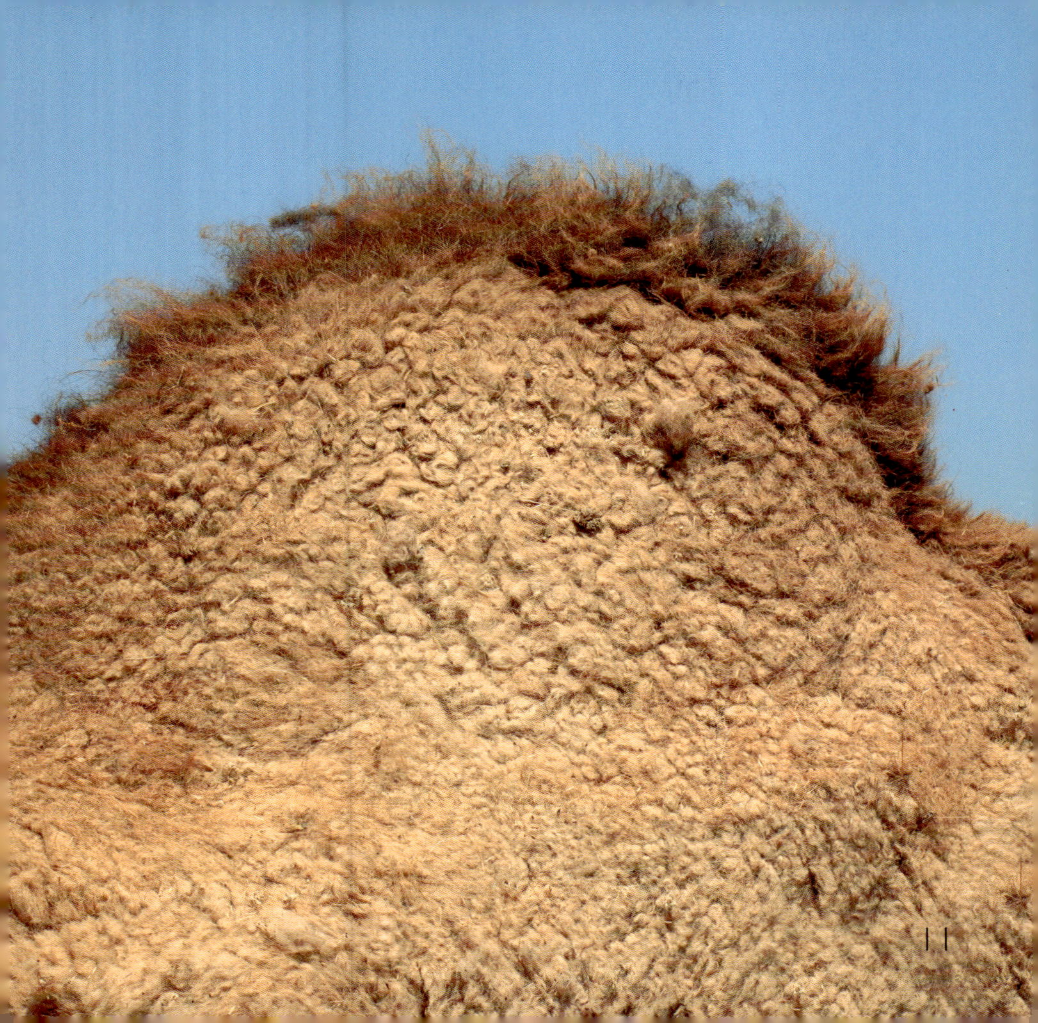

I am a camel.

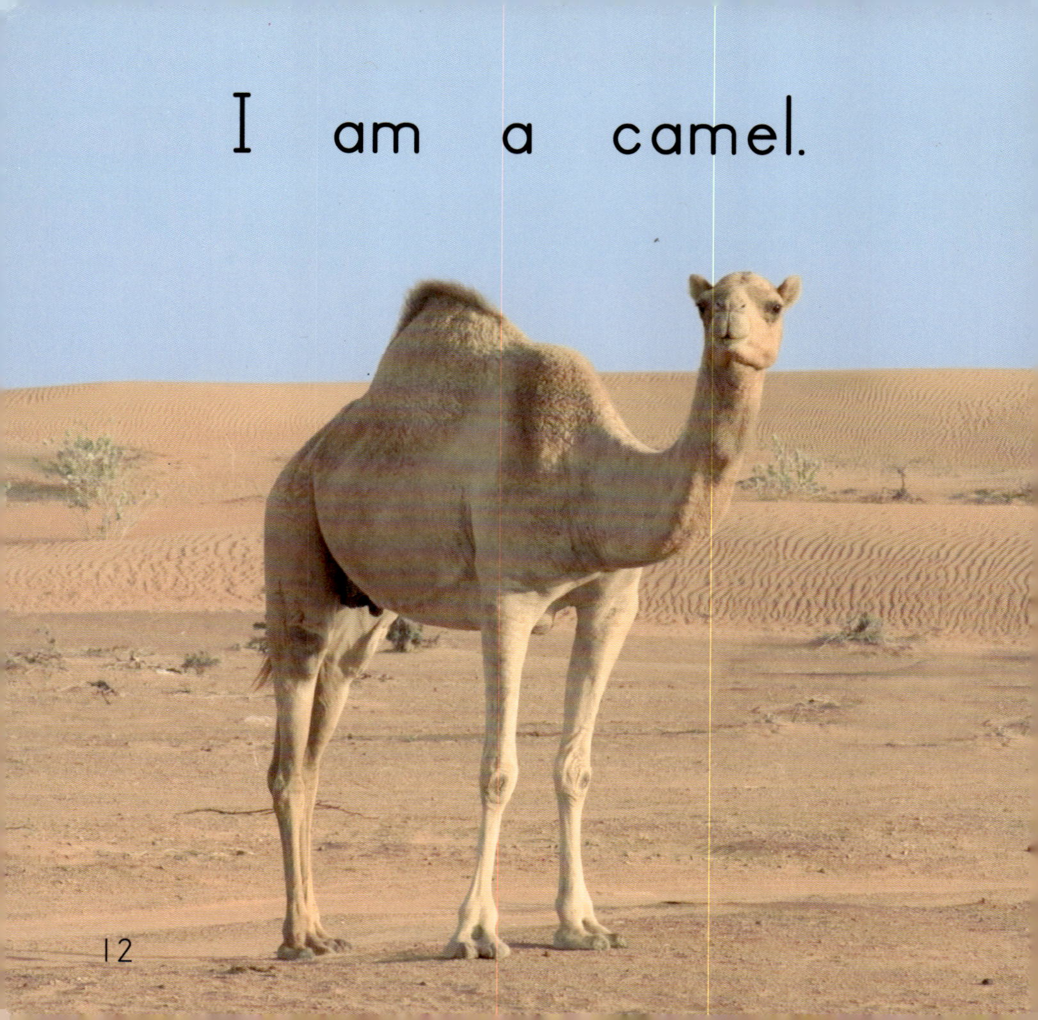